AUSTRALIA

 **Marshall Cavendish**
Benchmark

New York

Written by: Peter North and Susan McKay
Editor: Peter Mavrikis, Cheryl Sim
Publisher: Michelle Bisson
Series Designer: Benson Tan

Photo research by Thomas Khoo

Originated and designed by Marshall Cavendish International (Asia) Pte Ltd
Copyright © 2011 Marshall Cavendish International (Asia) Pte Ltd
Published by Marshall Cavendish Benchmark
An imprint of Marshall Cavendish Corporation
All rights reserved.

This publication represents the opinions and views of the authors based on
Peter North and Susan McKay's personal experience, knowledge, and research.
The information in this book serves as a general guide only. The authors and
publisher have used their best efforts in preparing this book and disclaim liability
rising directly and indirectly from the use and application of this book.

Other Marshall Cavendish Offices:
Marshall Cavendish International (Asia) Pte Ltd, 1 New Industrial Road,
Singapore 536196 ● Marshall Cavendish International (Thailand) Co Ltd.
253 Asoke, 12th Flr, Sukhumvit 21 Road, Klongtoey Nua, Wattana,
Bangkok 10110, Thailand ● Marshall Cavendish (Malaysia) Sdn Bhd,
Times Subang, Lot 46, Subang Hi-Tech Industrial Park, Batu Tiga,
40000 Shah Alam, Selangor Darul Ehsan, Malaysia

Marshall Cavendish is a trademark of Times Publishing Limited.
All websites were available and accurate when this book was sent to press.

Library of Congress Cataloging-in-Publication Data
North, Peter, 1943-
Australia / Peter North and Susan McKay.
p. cm. — (Welcome to my country)
Summary: "An overview of the history, geography, government, economy,
language, people, and culture of Australia. Includes numerous color photos,
a detailed map, useful facts, and detailed resource section"
—Provided by publisher.
Includes index.
ISBN 978-1-60870-150-6
1. Australia—Juvenile literature. I. McKay, Susan, 1972- II. Title.
DU96.N674 2011
994—dc22   2009051175

Printed in Malaysia
135642

PHOTO CREDITS

Alamy/Bes Stock: 7 (bottom), 16, 30, 34, 35, 37 (top), 39, 40
Art Directors & TRIP Photo Library: 26
Bes Stock: 24
Dave G. Houser/Houserstock: 9, 27, 31, 36
Getty Images: 3 (top), 8 (all), 17, 21, 25, 32, 33, 37 (bottom)
Hutchinson Library: 1, 4
Lonely Planet Images: 28
Photolibrary: cover, 2, 3 (centre), 3 (bottom), 5, 6, 7 (top), 10,
    13, 18, 22, 26
Richard l'Anson: 23, 41, 45
Topham Picturepoint: 11, 12, 14, 15 (all), 19, 20, 29 (all), 38

Contents

Words that appear in the glossary are printed in **boldface** type the first time they occur in the text.

A park guide cares for an orphaned kangaroo.

Welcome to Australia!

Many people imagine Australia as a large island with good weather all year round. More than half the country is covered in desert, but Australia has **temperate** and **tropical** climates, too. Let's learn all about the country called **Down Under** and the history of the people who live there.

Most Australian cities are along the coast, so the beach is never far away!

The Flag of Australia

The Australian flag carries the stars of the Southern Cross. This **constellation** is only visible in the **southern hemisphere** where Australia is located. The flag of the **United Kingdom** appears in the top left corner.

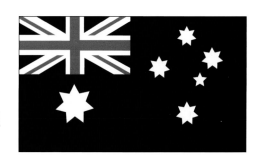

The Land

Australia is almost as large as the United States, not including Alaska. Most people live in the big cities along the coastal regions of the country.

Sydney, Melbourne, Brisbane, and Perth are all located along the Australian coast. The land formations change from region to region. Hardly anyone lives in the dry, central region known as the **outback**, or **bush**.

The eastern and southern coasts, northern Australia, and

Uluru, or Ayers Rock, is a large sandstone rock in the Northern Territory. It is a sacred site for the **Aborigines**, Australia's original inhabitants.

the southwestern region have rich, fertile land that is good for farming.

Most of Australia is very flat. The highest mountain is Mount Kosciusko at 7,310 feet (2,228 meters). It is located in the Great Dividing Range that runs along the eastern coast.

The Murray is the longest river in Australia. It snakes through the state of New South Wales, collecting rainfall off the mountain slopes.

The Great Barrier Reef is the world's largest coral reef. Corals live in warm, clear waters, such as those off the shores of tropical Queensland.

Spring flowers cover the land in Western Australia.

Seasons

Australia is in the southern hemisphere, where summer lasts from December to February and the winter months run from June to August. The climates of different regions range from dry and hot, to mild and wet.

This giant termite mound is made of mud. It is home to millions of termites—tiny antlike insects that feed on wood.

Trees, shrubs, and flowers found in Australia's deserts are very hardy plants that can survive extreme weather conditions.

It would take several people to form a ring around the thick trunk of this baobab tree!

Plants and Animals

Australia's famous animals include emus, kangaroos, koalas, and opossums. These mammals are known as **marsupials**. The mothers carry their babies in a pouch for months.

Special features help Australia's plants survive in its dry climate. Long roots help the eucalyptus tree seek out water. The baobab tree stores water in its thick trunk.

History

Australia's Original Settlers

The Aborigines came from Asia about forty thousand to fifty thousand years ago and were the first people to settle in Australia. The men hunted land animals and fished. The women gathered seeds, roots, and berries. When the Europeans first arrived, there were about half a million Aborigines living across Australia.

Boomerangs are V-shaped throwing clubs used by Aboriginal hunters. After it is thrown, the curved shape of the boomerang propels it back to its original position for easy retrieval.

Eighteen years after claiming Australia, the British establish a colony at Sydney Cove.

The Europeans Arrive

Just over two hundred years ago, European sailors landed on
the coasts of Australia. In 1770, British explorer James Cook
claimed the eastern coast of Australia for his king, George III.
For many years afterward, Britain sent **convicts** there. New
settlements were also established on the southern coast of
Australia and on the island of Tasmania.

In the early 1800s, the new settlers began exploring Australia on camels.

A Land of New Possibilities

Before long, **immigrants** were coming to Australia in large numbers, mainly from England and Ireland. These immigrants introduced new ways of farming and mining. They even brought a new animal with them in 1810—the sheep! Soon, Australia was a rich country with a successful wool industry. Australia had become a land with many new possibilities.

The Commonwealth of Australia

At the beginning of the twentieth century, there were six Australian territories, called colonies, inhabited by immigrants. In 1901, they joined to form a **federation** called the Commonwealth of Australia. Australia still had strong links with Britain, and Australians fought alongside the British in World Wars I and II. The Australian and New Zealand soldiers who fought in these wars were called ANZACs (Australian and New Zealand Army Corps).

This memorial in Brisbane is dedicated to the ANZAC soldiers who died fighting during World War I.

These young men from London came to Sydney in 1959. They were two of the many Europeans who settled in Australia.

Immigration

Since World War II, Australia has encouraged immigration. Today, Australia is known as a country of immigrants because many people living there were born elsewhere.

Matthew Flinders (1774—1814)

Matthew Flinders was a famous English explorer. In 1801, he proved that Australia was a single landmass by sailing all the way around the coast. At that time, Australia was known as **New Holland**. He suggested renaming it *Australia*, from the Latin word *australis*, meaning "southern."

Matthew Flinders

Caroline Chisholm (1808—1877)

In the early 1800s, poor women from Britain came to Australia to find a better life. Many of them had no money and were homeless. Caroline Chisholm set up the Female Immigrants' Home to help those women. Soon, she was known across the country as "the immigrant's friend." She helped more than ten thousand women.

Caroline Chisholm

The Government and the Economy

Government

Australia is divided into six states and two territories. Its government is divided into three sections—the town and city councils, the state and territory governments, and the federal government, which is based in Canberra, the capital city.

The New Parliament House was opened in 1988 and is located in Canberra. The building is designed in the shape of a boomerang.

Kevin Rudd was elected prime minister of Australia in 2007.

Australia's government is run by two houses of elected members—the House of Representatives and the Senate. Together, they decide on laws and government policies. The **prime minister** is the leader of the government and the country. He or she chooses politicians from either house to form a group called the **cabinet**. Each cabinet member, called a minister, is in charge of one area of government. These ministers advise the prime minister.

These rows of cattle in holding pens will eventually be sold at market auctions.

Agriculture

In the 1800s, the main industry in Australia was sheep farming. Today, Australia is still the world's largest wool-producing country. Cattle farming is important too and produces beef for both the nation and for export. Some cattle ranches stretch for miles and miles. Teams of men, trucks, and even helicopters are used to round up the herds.

Industry

In the nineteenth century, ships took months to bring goods to Australia, forcing Australians to make the things they needed for themselves. The Australian manufacturing industry began in this way.

Mining

Australia contains many natural resources. Gold, coal, iron ore, copper, tin, and nickel are mined in many regions. Under the ocean, natural gas is drilled and sold to other countries.

Iron ore is one of the major minerals found in Western Australia, along with gold, tin, coal, and diamonds.

People and Lifestyle

More Travelers Arrive!

Since the first settlers arrived, many immigrants have moved to Australia. Most people emigrated from Britain, but others traveled from Italy, Greece, China, Vietnam, and Lebanon. The original people of Australia, the Aborigines, make up a very small part of the population.

Immigrant Australians and Aborigines have not always been friends, but the situation has begun to improve.

Many Chinese immigrants live in the part of Sydney called Chinatown.

A Melting Pot

In Australia, many races of people live together in one land. The government has introduced a **policy** called **multiculturalism**, which encourages ethnic groups to live peacefully with one another.

Many immigrants from Asian countries arrived in Australia in the 1970s. Today, most Australian cities have large Asian communities.

Family Life

Most Australians live in homes in a town or city not far from the coast. Outdoor activities are popular with Australians, and the sunny climate allows them to visit the beach as often as they can.

Going to the beach is a favorite weekend activity enjoyed by many Australian families.

Australians take pride in their homes, like this man who is painting his fence.

Australia is a big country with a fairly small population, so most of the houses in the cities are large, with gardens at the front and back. Australians are very friendly with their neighbors, and most people know each other.

Australians are proud of their homes, and they take care of them well. Weekend projects might include a home improvement job, mowing the lawn, or working in the garden.

Education

All Australian children must attend school, starting at either five or six years of age. They attend primary school and secondary school. Primary school lasts six years. Students then go to secondary school, which lasts another six years.

Most schools in the country are run by the government and are free. Some parents send their children to private schools, which charge tuition fees.

Children who live in **rural** areas must take a bus to and from school.

Most Australian children have to wear a school uniform.

After secondary school, students can further their education by attending technical institutions, community colleges, or universities.

Australian schools offer activities such as drama, debating, and music, after school. Sports are also popular. Students can join clubs to play Australian Rules football, hockey, netball, and cricket. Australian Rules football is also called "Aussie Rules" and has elements of football, rugby, and basketball.

Religion

Christianity came to Australia with the European settlers, and Catholicism and Anglicanism are the main religions of the country today.

Before the Europeans arrived, the Aborigines practiced their own religion. They believed the spirits of their ancestors lived in the trees, water holes, and rocks. Some Aborigines today still hold this belief.

These are historic Aboriginal graves marked with poles to honor family members.

Sydney has many churches. This is St. Mary's, a Roman Catholic cathedral.

The Arrival of Christianity

The Europeans brought Christian beliefs with them from other countries and built churches all over Australia. Some of the first buildings in a town were churches. Immigrants from other countries brought their own religions, too. Today, there are Jews, Hindus, Buddhists, and Sikhs in Australia.

Language

A Mixture of Languages

The main Australian language is English, spoken by most citizens with an accent handed down by the original settlers from England and Ireland. Immigrants from European and Asian countries brought their own languages with them. Over the years, Australians have adopted some Aboriginal words, such as *Illawarra*, meaning "place by the sea."

People from countries all over the world have settled in Australia and it is common to see signs that are written in different languages.

Australian Stories

Traditional Australian stories tell of the lives of the people who lived in the outback. A man named A. B. "Banjo" Paterson wrote interesting stories about the outback. He also wrote Australia's unofficial anthem, *Waltzing Matilda*.

The stories of the outback are still being told by modern-day writers, such as Australian Julia Leigh. Born in Sydney in 1970, Leigh wrote the international bestseller *The Hunter*, which has been translated into six languages.

Peter Carey won the 1988 Booker Prize for Fiction for his book *Oscar and Lucinda*.

In 1973, Patrick White was the first Australian to win the Nobel Prize for Literature.

Arts

Painting

The oldest paintings in Australia were done by the Aborigines. They decorated cave walls with pictures of animals and people using natural materials, such as charcoal.

European settlers brought their own style of painting to Australia. Many famous Australian artists now mix the two styles together.

A hiker inspects Aboriginal artwork found on the walls of Warumba Cave in Queensland.

The Sydney Opera House is in front of the Harbour Bridge. People in Sydney call the bridge "The Coat Hanger" because of its unusual shape.

Architecture

The Harbour Bridge and the Sydney Opera House are two of Australia's most famous structures. Sydney Harbour is divided by a waterway. The Harbour Bridge joins the two halves of the harbor together.

The Sydney Opera House is one of the busiest theaters in the world, presenting plays, operas, musicals, and ballets. Architects and craftspeople took fourteen years to complete it.

Music

Australians love making music! Have you heard of the rock bands the Bee Gees, AC/DC, Midnight Oil, and INXS? Or how about the opera singers Dame Nellie Melba and Dame Joan Sutherland, known as two of the world's best performers? These musical stars all come from Australia.

Australian singer-songwriter Delta Goodrem has achieved eight No. 1 singles in her country, more than any other local singer.

Australia was filmed around the country and starred native actor and actress Hugh Jackman and Nicole Kidman. The movie's director, Baz Luhrmann, is also Australian.

Films

The 2008 film *Australia* is one of the most recent Australian movies to be an international box office hit. *Crocodile Dundee*, about an outback man who moves to New York City, is probably the best-known Australian film. Australians Nicole Kidman, Cate Blanchett, Geoffrey Rush, and Mel Gibson have all won Academy Awards, or Oscars, in Hollywood.

Many locally produced movies are made in Australia. Every year, Australian filmmakers go to the Cannes Film Festival in France to show their films.

Leisure Time

A Love of the Outdoors

Australia's climate is perfect for spending time outdoors. Australians love to watch and play sports, such as cricket and Australian Rules football. Fishing is a very popular Australian pastime. It gives people a chance to get away from the hustle and bustle of the city. The great thing is, the water is never far away!

The waters of the Northern Territory are popular with fishing fans.

Hikers on a bush walk through Coburg National Park in Australia's Northern Territory.

Outdoor Adventures

Many Australians like to go **bush-walking**, and there are trails throughout most of the country.

Most Australians live near the coast. They love swimming and surfing. The country is surrounded by water, and there are plenty of great surfing spots on the coast. There is even a beach in Australia called Surfer's Paradise!

Sports

Cricket is one of the best-loved sports in Australia. Children and adults play this game in backyards, fields, and **sporting ovals**. Australian Rules football is the main winter sport.

Horse racing is also a popular spectator sport. The Melbourne Cup, held in November, is the biggest horse racing event in Australia.

On Melbourne Cup day, the racetrack is surrounded with excited spectators. In the rest of the country, people watch the race on television.

Australian Champions

One of the most famous Australian sports champions is golfer Greg Norman. In 1971, Yvonne Cawley became the first Aboriginal tennis player to win the Wimbledon championship. She won it again in 1980. Former world champion Lleyton Hewitt won the Grand Slam in 2001 and the Wimbledon title in 2002. In swimming, Ian Thorpe has won five Olympic gold medals—the biggest haul by an Australian athlete.

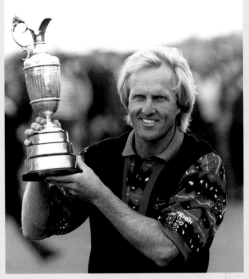

Golfer Greg Norman has won many international competitions.

Tennis player Lleyton Hewitt has won the Grand Slam and Wimbledon.

Holidays

Christmas is the biggest holiday on the Australian calendar. It falls at the beginning of summer and marks the end of the school year. (Remember that seasons are different in the southern hemisphere.) Most people celebrate the holiday with a family lunch of turkey. Some people celebrate with a barbecue on the beach.

ANZAC Day is on April 25. It is a day to remember the ANZAC soldiers who lost their lives in World Wars I and II. **Veteran** soldiers parade through the streets wearing their uniforms.

The ANZAC Day parade. These nurses are wearing a sprig of rosemary, the herb of remembrance, above their medals.

The log chop is a race to see who can chop a log in half the quickest.

Australia Day is celebrated on January 26. It marks the day the first group of immigrants arrived in the country. People all over Australia celebrate by singing the national anthem and setting off fireworks!

Every year, each state holds an agricultural show. Prizes are awarded for the best cows, the biggest bulls, and the sheep with the finest **fleece**. Other contests include the log chop and the high pole, where loggers race to chop the top off tree trunks while balancing on narrow planks.

Food

Immigrants brought national dishes with them, and today foods from many other countries are available—pasta from Italy, olives from Greece, curries from India, and **kebabs** from Turkey. Traditional Aboriginal foods include wattle seeds, bunya nuts, and fruits like the Quandong and Kakadu plum. Animal and plant foods that are native to Australia are commonly referred to as **bush tucker**.

Wichetty grubs are fat, white, sluglike creatures. Usually eaten raw or lightly cooked, the grub is popular in trendy Sydney restaurants!

There are plenty of public barbecue pits in Australia.

In the outback, food is very simple. One type of traditional food is **damper**. Damper is flour and sugar mixed with water, cooked over an open fire.

During the summer, many Australians cook on a barbecue pit. They call it a *barbie*. The most popular barbecued foods are meats and seafood. Barbecued vegetables are delicious, too. A barbecue on the beach is a popular way to celebrate Christmas.

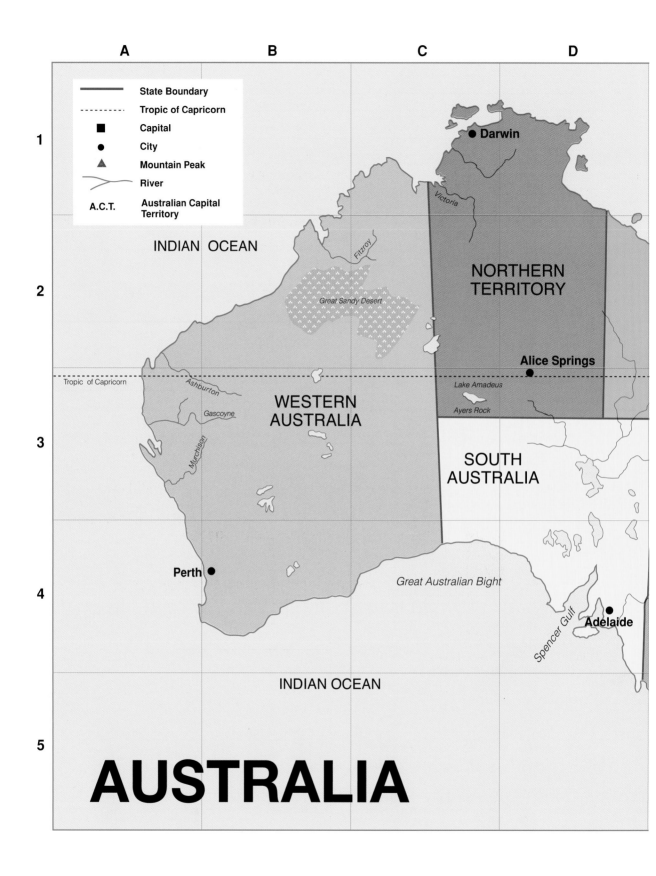

AUSTRALIA

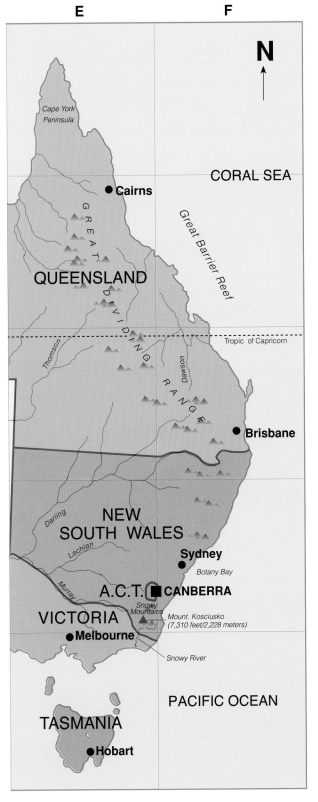

E	F

N ↑

Cape York
Peninsula

CORAL SEA

● **Cairns**

Great Barrier Reef

G R E A T   D I V I D I N G   R A N G E

QUEENSLAND

Thomson

Dawson

Tropic of Capricorn

● **Brisbane**

NEW
SOUTH WALES

Darling

Lachlan

Murray

Sydney

Botany Bay

A.C.T. ■ **CANBERRA**

Snowy Mountains

VICTORIA

▲ *Mount. Kosciusko
(7,310 feet/2,228 meters)*

● **Melbourne**

Snowy River

PACIFIC OCEAN

TASMANIA

● **Hobart**

Adelaide D4
Alice Springs D3
Amadeus, Lake C3
Ashburton River A3
Australian Capital
  Territory
  (A.C.T.) E4
Ayers Rock C3

Botany Bay F4
Brisbane F3

Cairns E2
Canberra E4
Cape York
  Peninsula E1
Coral Sea F2

Darling River E4
Darwin C1
Dawson River F3

Fitzroy River C2

Gascoyne River B3
Great Australian Bight
  C4
Great Barrier Reef F2
Great Dividing Range
  E2–F3
Great Sandy
  Desert B2–C2

Hobart E5

Indian Ocean A2–B5

Lachlan River E4

Melbourne E5
Mount Kosciusko E4
Murchison River A3
Murray River E4

New South Wales E4
Northern Territory C2

Pacific Ocean F5
Perth B4

Queensland E2

Snowy Mountains
  E4
Snowy River E5
South Australia
  C3–D3
Spencer Gulf D4
Sydney F4

Tasmania E5
Thomson River E3
Tropic of Capricorn
  A3

Victoria E4
Victoria River C1

Western Australia B3

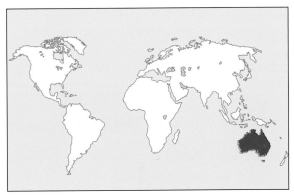

Quick Facts

Official Name Australia

Capital Canberra

Official Language English

Population 21,262,641

Land Area 2.9 million square miles (7.7 million square kilometers)

States New South Wales, Queensland, South Australia, Tasmania, Victoria, Western Australia

Territories Australian Capital Territory, Northern Territory

Major Cities Adelaide, Brisbane, Cairns, Canberra, Darwin, Melbourne, Perth, Sydney

Highest Point Mount Kosciusko (7,310 feet/2,228 meters)

Major River Murray River

Main Religions Anglican, Roman Catholic

Major Festivals Australia Day (January 26), ANZAC Day (April 25), Christmas (December 25)

National Animals Emu, kangaroo

Currency Australian dollar (AUD 1.14 = U.S. $1 in 2010)

This sign warns that camels, wombats, or kangaroos may be crossing ahead.

Glossary

Aborigines: The original people of Australia.

boomerang: A V-shaped hunting weapon used by the Aborigines.

bush: An area of forest, desert, or scrubland outside the main cities.

bush tucker: Any type of plant or animal from Australia that is eaten for food.

bush-walking: Hiking in the bush.

cabinet: Group of government ministers.

constellation: A group of stars forming patterns in the sky.

convict: A person who is serving a prison sentence.

damper: A dumpling made from flour, sugar, and water.

Down Under: Another name for the country of Australia.

federation: A group of governmental organizations.

fleece: A sheep's coat.

immigrant: A person that moves to another country.

kebab: Chunks of meat and vegetables on a skewer or wrapped in bread.

marsupial: An animal whose young live in its pouch.

multiculturalism: Including many different countries and cultures.

New Holland: The former name of Australia.

outback: The central area of Australia.

policy: A strategy or rule made by the government.

prime minister: The political leader of a country.

rural: Relating to the countryside, away from towns and cities.

southern hemisphere: The southern half of Earth.

sporting oval: Field built for sports activities and competitions.

temperate: Having a climate with four seasons.

tropical: Having a climate with hot, sticky, wet weather all year round.

United Kingdom: The collective name for England, Scotland, Wales, and Northern Ireland.

veteran: A former soldier.

witchetty grub: A small, white, sluglike creature.

For More Information

Books

Boraas, Tracey. *Australia*. Mankato, MN: Capstone Press, 2006.

Kalman, Bobbie. *Explore Australia and Oceania*. New York: Crabtree Publishing Company, 2007.

Lester, Alison. *Are We There Yet?: A Journey around Australia*. San Diego, CA: Kane/Miller Book Publishers, 2005.

Lewin, Ted and Betsy. *Top to Bottom Down Under*. New York: HarperCollins Children's Books, 2005.

McCollum, Sean. *Australia*. Minneapolis, MN: Lerner Publications, 2007.

Sasek, Miroslav. *This is Australia*. New York: Universe Publishing, 2009.

Stockdale, Stephanie. *Sidney Visits Australia*. Bloomington, IN: AuthorHouse, 2009.

DVDs

Alone Across Australia. (Direct Cinema Limited, 2005).

Australia. (20th Century Fox, 2009).

Discovery Atlas: Australia Revealed (Discovery Channel, 2007).

Wildest Islands of Australia. (Goldhil Home Media, 2008).

Websites

library.thinkquest.org/28994/index.html

Learn more about Australia's history, geography, cities, culture and more.

www.kidcyber.com.au/topics/animals.htm

An extensive A-Z directory of all kinds of animals found in Australia.

www.nationalgeographic.com/earthpulse/reef/reef1_flash.html

Go on a virtual tour to the world-famous Great Barrier Reef in Australia.

www.zoomschool.com/school/Australia/

An informative site where you can even learn to create your own piece of Australian Aboriginal art.

Index